Contents

Some words are in bold, **like this**. You can find them in the glossary on page 23.

An orangutan is a **mammal**.

Many mammals have hairy bodies and feed their babies milk.

chimpanzee

Orangutans belong to a group of mammals called **apes**.

Chimpanzees and gorillas are also types of apes.

What do orangutans look like?

Orangutans have large bodies that are covered in long, red-brown hair.

They have very long, strong arms.

cheek

pouch

Male orangutans are bigger than females.

An adult male has big cheeks and a baggy **pouch** around its neck.

Where do orangutans live?

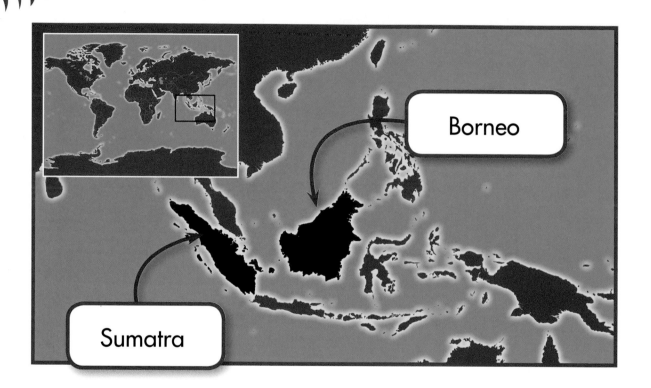

Borneo

Sumatra

Orangutans live on the islands of Borneo and Sumatra in South East Asia.

They live in the **rainforests** that grow on the islands.

Orangutans spend most of their time high up in the rainforest trees.

They do not come down to the ground very often.

What do orangutans do in the day?

An orangutan wakes up when the Sun rises.

It has a snack of fruit for breakfast.

After breakfast, the orangutan has a short rest before it starts the day.

Then it spends most of the day looking for food among the trees.

What do orangutans eat and drink?

Orangutans mainly eat fruit, leaves, and other parts of plants.

An orangutan picks a fruit, then peels it with its teeth and **rubbery** lips.

It rains every day in the **rainforest**.

When an orangutan feels thirsty, it scoops up rainwater from a hole in a tree to drink.

How do orangutans move about?

vine

An orangutan rocks on a branch or **vine**.

It does this until it is close enough to grab another branch or vine.

hand

The orangutan always holds on to a tree with at least one hand and one foot.

Its hands and feet are shaped like hooks for grabbing hold of the branches.

Do orangutans live alone?

Male orangutans usually live on their own.

They do not help to look after young orangutans.

A young orangutan lives with its
mother until it is about eight years old.

Its mother teaches it where to find food
in the **rainforest**.

Are orangutans noisy?

A male orangutan can be very noisy.

He can puff up his neck **pouch** and make a loud roaring sound.

This sound can be heard far away in
the **rainforest**.

It warns other orangutans to stay away
from the tree where the male is feeding.

What do orangutans do at night?

nest

In the evening, an orangutan builds a nest in the trees with leaves and twigs.

The nest is where the orangutan sleeps.

Baby orangutans are born in the nest
at night.

When they are older, their mother
shows them how to make nests.

Orangutan body map

hand

fur

arm

eye

ear

cheek

throat pouch

Glossary

 **ape** large, human-like mammal, such as an orangutan or a chimpanzee

 **mammal** animal that feeds its babies milk. Most mammals have hair or fur.

 **pouch** baggy piece of skin

 **rainforest** thick forest with very tall trees and a lot of rain

 **rubbery** soft and bendy

 **vine** long, dangling plant that grows in the rainforest

Find out more

Books

Rainforest Animals (Focus on Habitats), Stephen Savage
  (Wayland, 2006)
Orangutans (Animals in Danger)
  (Ticktock Media Ltd, 2006)

Websites

www.orangutans-sos.org/kids/orangutan_facts/
http://kids.nationalgeographic.com/Animals/CreatureFeature/
  Orangutan

Index